I0445436

GAIN WISDOM, GAIN WEALTH

Also by Robert Mulindwa

Created for Success:
Finding God's Will, Our Purpose,
and True Happiness

Rediscovering Identity:
You Are The Image Of God

GAIN WISDOM, GAIN WEALTH

The Wise You Is the Path to Prosperity

ROBERT MULINDWA

KINGDOM COME

PUBLISHING

KINGDOM
COME

PUBLISHING

Copyright © 2025 by Robert Mulwinda
All rights reserved.
Published by Kingdom Come Publishing
Nashville, TN

No part of this book may be reproduced in any manner
without written permission except in the case of brief
quotations embodied in critical articles and reviews.

For information about special discounts for bulk purchases or
author interviews, appearances, and speaking engagements
please contact:

www.RobertMulindwa.com

MulindwaRobert123@gmail.com

First Edition

ISBN eBook	979-8-9876653-6-7
ISBN paperback	979-8-9876653-7-4
ISBN hardcover	979-8-9876653-8-1

Library of Congress Control Number: 2025926103

Cover design by Robert Mulindwa
Images care of www.Pixabay.com
Edited, book and page design, production by Rodney Miles

GAIN WISDOM TO GAIN WEALTH

*for she is more profitable than silver
   and yields better returns than gold.*

*She is more precious than rubies;
   nothing you desire can compare with her.*

—*Proverbs 3:14-15*

To the Simple, the Learned,
and the Understanding.

THE I AM MOVEMENT

Awakening the Divine Identity Within

Before wealth manifests in your hands, it must first be awakened in your identity. This is the heartbeat of the I AM Movement—a call for humanity to remember the forgotten truth of who we are.

The most powerful force in your life is the consciousness behind the words "I AM." Whatever follows those two words becomes a command to the universe, a decree to the mind, and a blueprint for your reality.

Most people try to change their circumstances while their identity remains unchanged. They say "I am not enough, I am broke, I am unworthy," and the world faithfully reflects their internal declaration.

The I AM Movement restores the original revelation: **You do not become wealthy by effort alone. You become wealthy by identity.** Your outer world rearranges itself to match who you believe you are at your core.

The Movement is built on three pillars:

1. Identity Precedes Destiny

You cannot rise beyond the self-image you carry. When you shift your identity, your decisions, behaviors, and opportunities shift instantly.

2. Consciousness Creates Experience

What you consistently declare "I AM" becomes the state your life conforms to. Affirmation is not wishful thinking—it is identity alignment.

3. Divinity Is Within, Not Outside You

The spark of the Infinite lives in you. Wisdom is recognizing this truth. Wealth is expressing this truth in your decisions, actions, and stewardship.

***

*The purpose of the I AM Movement is simple: **to awaken the sleeping divinity within man and restore him to his rightful dominion.***

*When you declare **I AM**, you are not describing your condition — you are **activating your potential.***

*And when wisdom shapes what you say after "I AM," **wealth becomes the natural consequence.***

CONTENTS

PREFACE

I WILL ALLUDE to a quote by Warren Wiersbe, an American clergy:

"We are living in the information age, but we certainly aren't living in the age of wisdom. Many people who are wizards with their computers seem to be amateurs when it comes to making a success out of their lives."

This is so true in today's world—a world characterized by rapid change, constant noise, and clutter that constitute unending distractions. The world today has a lot of people who are unconscious, unaware of the fundamental Truth, so to speak. The diligent search for knowledge, understanding, and wisdom, has often taken the back seat, as the masses focus on the pursuit of material success, fleeting pleasures, and secular knowledge.

Now, it's important to note that there is a distinction between knowledge and wisdom. It's also true that there exists a difference between understanding and wisdom. There is such a thing as a knowledgeable person without understanding and wisdom.

- *Knowledge* is the warehousing of information or facts.

- *Understanding* is the mental comprehension of facts.

- *Wisdom* is the correct application of facts in daily life. For instance, a smoking doctor demonstrates a lack of wisdom.

The title of this book, *"Wisdom is Supreme,"* is predicated on a primordial proverb that emphasizes the unmatched value of wisdom. For wisdom isn't just one quality among many, but the foundation upon which long life, health, riches, and honor are built.

And as the epigraph in the front of this book states:

"It's more profitable than silver,
yields better returns than gold,
more precious than rubies,
and nothing you desire can
compare."

This postulates that its value is beyond compare.

Since the dawn of time, sages, philosophers, prophets, and thinkers all suggest enduring success, genuine fulfillment, and inner peace do not derive from external accomplishments, but from knowledge, understanding, and wisdom. Why? Because wisdom, once grasped, dictates every choice, action, and decision-making, resulting in a life of realized potential, integrity, and true success—lasting success.

In this book, you will not be feasting on theoretical knowledge, but rather provided a practical guide rooted in divine wisdom—wisdom that not only leads to individual success but to a deeper relationship with our Creator, our inner core, others, and the world around us.

"Wisdom is Supreme" is a clarion call that underscores what truly matters, as in investing our time, energy, and resources in acquiring understanding, no matter the cost. Regardless of background or standing, simple or learned, parent or teacher, professional or leader, or simply someone seeking clarity and direction in life, this book will bring to light the timeless truth that has guided wise men and women for centuries.

Now, let us embark on this journey together to discover why wisdom is supreme, and why it is worth the weight in gold to gain understanding.

References

https://wiersbe.com/

https://enduringword.com/bible-commentary/proverbs-1

INTRODUCTION

"Wisdom is supreme; so acquire wisdom. And whatever you may acquire, gain understanding."

—Proverbs 4:7

THE MAXIM above clearly implies that fame, power, or money are not the principle thing, but wisdom. Every human being possesses the potential to live fully and fulfilled through wise choices, actions, and decisions; however, most people fall short. Why? The sociological programing resulting from our experiences, education, and environment disrupts our *true* intelligence—the original spiritual intelligence.

What we call *education* was designed to mass produce obedient workers, lacking in innovation and creativity. This results in the many serving a few, creating an imbalance where these few have become masters who *materialize* the spiritual. The few recognize that "As a man thinketh in his heart so is he"(Proverbs 23:7).

Wisdom is the understanding of this fundamental truth that thoughts are things, and each human has the inherent ability to originate thoughts of the things they desire. Higher thinking is spiritual in nature.

Mankind was created in the image and likeness of the Creator. Recognizing one's creative ability through the transformation of the mind, and rejecting conformity to the world is key to health, wealth, and wellbeing. This is wisdom. It is the understanding that spiritual things or higher thought is the realty to be expressed in the physical. It is the discernment that thoughts are things, and whatever one thinks becomes their realty.

In theological lingual, heaven is the realty, and earth is the expression of heaven. And wisdom is understanding that the spiritual is superior to the physical. Hence, heaven gives meaning to earth, and earth gives expression to heaven. This is wisdom, and the search for wisdom is not new. Philosophers, biblical prophets, sages of the east, and modern day though leaders have been at the forefront of the pursuit of wisdom.

At its root, wisdom is not just intelligence or knowledge. Why? Because knowledge is warehousing of facts, while wisdom is the ability to apply that knowledge in a way that is beneficial and meaningful. Wisdom provides one a lens to visualize the world in crystal clear fashion, resulting in sound decision-making and purposeful living.

A wise person chooses:

- insight over information,

- mind over matter,

- spiritual over material.

Because he or she understands the invisible is realty while the visible is the expression of that realty.

This book was inspired by the ancient text, Proverbs 4:7; "Wisdom is supreme, therefore get wisdom. Though it costs all you have, get understanding." This verse clearly demonstrates that very few things if any are more valuable than wisdom. It is way more valuable than money, more precious than fame, power, or wealth, and outlasts temporary success.

Where wisdom is lacking, even what is considered a prosperous life by worldly standards crumbles under the weight of poor decision-making, misguided ambition, and lack of deeper insight. So why is wisdom costly? Because it calls for acknowledgment of one's deficiencies or knowledge gaps.

Seek it diligently, then, and search for it like a covetous man pursues riches.

Yet the greatest tragedy according to Wiersbe is that:

"There is so much noise that people can't hear the things they really need to hear. God is trying to get through to them with the voice of wisdom, but all they hear art the confused communication clutter, foolish voices that lead them farther away from the truth."

However, those who seek wisdom faithfully will find the rewards outweigh the cost. Where wisdom is, purpose is clear, resulting in effective and efficient decision-making, peace of mind, success, and significance.

In *Wisdom is Supreme*, we will dive into the principles that have stood the test of time in guiding wise individuals throughout history and how these can be of benefit in the present time. Practical insights and examples will be furnished in the coming chapters to help you in not only discerning wisdom, but to utilize it in positive, tangible ways.

The pursuit of wisdom is a lifelong journey that calls for commitment, consistency, and dedication. As you peruse the pages of this book, my hope and prayer is that you become inspired, such that the pursuit of wisdom is top priority in life. For wisdom will translate into riches, wealth, honor, and long life.

Per the ancient text of Proverbs 3: 13-15:

"Blessed are those who find wisdom, those who gain understanding, for she is more profitable than silver and yields better returns than gold. She is more precious than rubies; nothing you desire can compare with her."

—Proverbs 3:13-15

So let us embark on this journey of discerning why wisdom is the root that precedes the fruit.

References

https://biblehub.com/proverbs/4-7.htm

https://www.biblestudytools.com/bible-study/topical-studies/what-does-as-a-man-thinketh-so-is-he-mean-in-the-bible.html

https://enduringword.com/bible-commentary/proverbs-1

/ 1 /

UNDERSTANDING: THE FOUNDATION OF WISDOM

IN TODAY'S MODERN society the wisdom of God is not the center of attention, as the culture and education system focuses on secular knowledge. This is not accidental, but intentional as the knowledge of God which is the fundamental truth was erased out of the curriculum. It's evident that by sowing this iniquity, modern society is reaping a whirlwind of consequences. There are hundreds of TV channels for the individual to watch in this day and age. There are several social media and digital platforms serving as communication vehicles; however, not one is dedicated to the "Wisdom of God." Consequences for this deliberate practice are commonplace.

You may ask, "What are the consequences of removing God from educational and cultural settings?" According to Ezra Taft Benson, a former United States Secretary of Agriculture and religious leader:

_____

"Judging by its demoralized works, atheism has now quit advancing in this country simply because it has arrived. Not just rhetorically but actually- our country is in an ungodly mess. City streets are terrorized by crime; our biggest and most expensive campuses are paralyzed by nihilism and anarchy; with special license from the Supreme Court, theaters are boldly featuring sex

perversion, and the newsstands
are loaded with hardcore
pornography. Big name
investigating commissions have
told us all about riots, crime,
progress, and poverty, but
always in materialistic terms of
money, housing, social service
jobs, and birth control- without a
word about the possibilities for
personal moral self-restraint."

Clearly, we have a glaring tragedy in our society. Additionally, as many become learned in worldly things including science and philosophy, they consider themselves self-sufficient, trusting their knowledge instead of God. Now, due to their bias in worldly and secular knowledge, they challenge the existence of God for anything they can't prove and validate physically, mathematically, or scientifically. There is such a thing as knowledge without wisdom, but there can never be wisdom without knowledge. Why? Because wisdom is a revelation from God.

God the Creator is the *only* source of wisdom. As humans, we have an inherent tendency to place our trust in someone or something, or ourselves. However, Scripture exhorts us to trust in the Creator of the Universe.

An ancient Proverb (3:5-6) postulates:

"Trust in the Lord with all your heart and lean not on your own understanding: in all ways submit to Him, and He will make your paths straight."

—Proverbs 3:5-6

This clearly implies that we deliberately and intentionally decide to put our faith in Him concerning matters of understanding.

Jerry Bridges, an acclaimed author and speaker asserts that, "This trust is not the mere cold assent of enlightened judgment. It is trust... with all your heart. It is a childlike, unwavering confidence in our Father's well-proved wisdom, faithfulness, and love."

Therefore the foundation for gaining true understanding and wisdom is premised on the recognition of the sovereignty of God, and our place within His creation.

Hence:

"The fear of the Lord is the beginning of wisdom, and knowledge of the Holy One is understanding."

—Proverbs 9:10

To the casual eye, the statement, "fear of the Lord" can arouse a sense of intimidation, or even associate it with antiquity. In today's society fear is often associated with negative emotions such as terror, fright, or dread. However, in biblical lingual fear of the Lord doesn't imply a paralyzing fear, but rather a deep and great respect, reverence, and high esteem. This profound reverence is the controlling principle in seeking, searching, and acquiring wisdom. In depth, we will explore what it means to have a reverent fear of the Lord and how this is the beginning point to gaining wisdom. Also, we will explore practical examples of this principle, and how it relates to our present age, decision-making and personal development.

Authentic knowledge, understanding, and wisdom emerge from the fear of the Lord.

You may ask, "Who is God?" Attempting to define God is a tall order because He is infinite in every aspect, and definitions by nature prescribe boundaries of what is being defined. Nonetheless, I will allude to Scripture because it is here where God chooses to reveal whatever He desires about Himself to us. Isaiah 45:5-6 asserts:

"I am the Lord, and there is no other, apart from me there is no God. I will strengthen you, though you have not acknowledged me. So that from the rising of the sun to the place of its setting, men may know

there is none besides me. I am the
Lord and there is no other."

—Isaiah 45:5-6

This is one of the many verses in Scripture
that reveal to us who God is, necessitating a
fitting reverence that the created owes to the
Creator. Several definitions from several
writers pertaining to the fear of the Lord are as
below:

"But what is the fear of the Lord?
It is that affectionate reverence
by which the child of God bend
himself humbly and carefully to
his Father's law." (Bridges)

"A worshipping submission to
the God of the covenant."
(Kidner)

"The fear of the Lord ultimately expresses reverential submission to the Lord's will and thus characterizes a true worshiper." (Ross)

"The fear of the Lord signifies that religious reverence which every intelligent being owes to his Creator." (Clarke)

It's this respectful mindset where mankind acknowledges, understands, and reveres the Creator who establishes the beginning of wisdom. Without this first and controlling principle, wisdom can't progress further. Mankind can accomplish several things on his own, however no accomplishment will guarantee contentment and fulfillment without submission to the Most High. Therefore, human capacity, capability, and sagacity is not enough to gain true wisdom, but the fear of the Lord.

Bruce Waltke, an American Reformed Evangelical Professor, asserts that:

"What the alphabet is to reading, notes to reading music, and numerals to mathematics, the fear of the lord is to attaining the revealed knowledge of this book."

The book being referred to is the *Bible*.

Now, acquiring wisdom calls for transformation and renewing of one's mind, and turning away from darkness to light. Darkness is the ignorance due to lack of awareness, while light is knowledge of God, understanding, and wisdom.

Without the deep reverence of the Creator, we will lack in our efforts to seek and search for wisdom from the Ultimate Source. This process of pursuing wisdom involves our entire being—that is, spirit, soul, and body. Scripture exhorts us to pursue wisdom as one looking for silver and hidden treasure (Proverbs 2:4). This is corroborated by Clarke:

> "How do men seek money? What will they not do to get rich? Reader, seek the salvation of thy soul as earnestly as the covetous man seeks wealth, and be ashamed of thyself, if thou be less in earnest after true riches than he is after perishing wealth."

Let's consider the story of the wisest and wealthiest man in scripture, King Solomon. In his vision, God granted him the opportunity to ask for whatever he desired, a blank check is what we are talking about here. Solomon chose to have a discerning heart to govern and to distinguish between right and wrong; or between good and evil.

What? Are you kidding me?

This may be the response from most people in modern society because we have been programmed to believe that true success is defined by power, fame, nobility, and wealth—external achievements. However, Solomon understood that the most important thing was the wisdom to carry out his primary purpose in a way that honors God.

"Because you asked for wisdom, and not wealth, honor, or long life, I will give you what you asked for," said the Lord God. And not only that, also, "Shall I give you what you didn't ask for and that is long life, honor, and wealth."

Solomon's account clearly shows us that when we seek wisdom as the primary thing, the rest will be added to us.

"Therefore whoever hears these sayings of Mine, and does them, I will liken him to a wise man who built his house on the rock."

—Mathew 7:24

Our challenge in acquiring wisdom in today's world is the glut of information at our disposal. The marriage between the information age and digital age has procreated people so knowledgeable, but lacking in wisdom.

In the words of Warren Wiersbe:

"Fools are people who are ignorant of truth because they're dull and stubborn. Their problem isn't a low IQ or poor education; their problem is a lack of spiritual desire to seek and find God's wisdom."

Nonetheless, all hope is not lost, and the good news is that wisdom is available for anyone (irrespective of background, social status, race, religion, education status, ad infinitum) who genuinely and faithfully seeks it.

In his book, *The Wisdom Pyramid,* Brett McCracken refers to the old food pyramid that depicts how a balanced diet of good nutrition in the right proportions promotes a healthy body. Compare this to the option of feasting on junk food and its consequences. Brett McCracken asserts that we are in an epistemological crisis characterized by post-truth, alternative facts, fake news, and infotainment.

Post-truth is defined as, "relating to or denoting circumstances in which objective facts are less influential in shaping public opinions than appeals to emotion and personal belief." "Alternative facts" was a phrase used by Kellyanne Conway, then counselor to then President Donald Trump during a *Meet the Press* interview with Chuck Todd in January 2017. In the interview she defended proven-false statements made by the White House Press Secretary, Sean Spicer, as "alternative facts." This points to a bigger issue of curating our own experiences that speak to our preferred ideas and facts. Fake news speaks to the distrust in the media houses. Infotainment refers to the trivialization of the news into information and entertainment in a bid to increase ratings and clicks. This is where media houses make everything important, implying nothing is important.

Brett McCracken adds that:

"We are bombarded by a glut of content and information but have so little wisdom. I think we need guidance on heathier habits of knowledge intake. We need a wisdom pyramid. We need to think about what sorts of knowledge groups, and in what proportion, feed a healthy life of true wisdom and true joy."

The equalizer lies in embracing the truth of God such that there is a common denominator of what true wisdom is. The truth of God is the only truth, and it's spiritual in nature. Truth is factual, but not all facts are true. The fear of God is the foundation upon which to build all facts that define truth. This leads us to the Word of God in the Bible to serve as the controlling principle in gaining wisdom.

God is truth and His truth is wisdom. This truth of God is the spiritual law behind everything that is seen. Spiritual law is embedded in the super conscious. Wisdom lies in the understanding that the invisible is the realty, while the visible is the expression of it.

Now, as an example I will use parenting to demonstrate wise parenting premised on the fear of God. God-fearing parents will not only focus on raising good citizens, but recognize they are raising and nurturing lives entrusted to them by the Creator of the Universe. This kind of understanding shapes how the children are taught, guided, and disciplined. For instance, focus will be on instilling qualities of love, patience, kindness, faithfulness, honesty, and high respect for God, rather than academic excellence and material success. Parents will model this in their own daily life.

Therefore in raising children premised on the fear of God principle, parents will have equipped the children to embrace life with dignity, integrity, and wisdom, challenges withstanding. This is possible through practical steps such as:

- Acknowledging the sovereignty and existence of God.

- Studying the Word of God daily.

- Embracing a prayerful life.

- Recognizing the need for keeping company and making friends that are God-fearing.

- Freedom from pride and arrogance— that is, being humble and respectful.

The fear of the Lord is a timeless and relevant concept, for it is the controlling and foundational principle to gaining true wisdom. Total and complete trust in the Lord is a must. As humans we have an inherent tendency to be self-sufficient and self-dependent; however, for true wisdom that guarantees contentment, fulfillment, and lasting success, total trust and confidence in God is a requirement.

So what do we do?

"Trust in the Lord with all your
heart and lean not on your own
understanding; in all your ways
submit to him, and He will make
your paths straight. Do not be
wise in your own eyes; fear the
Lord and shun evil"

—Proverbs 3: 5-7

References

https://josephsmithfoundation.org/32-god-removed-what-is-the-consequence-of-removing-god-from-educational-settings-when-prophets-and-the-foun

https://mormonquotes.com/Ezra_Taft_Benson

https://www.reporter-times.com/story/lifestyle/faith/2021/07/09/examining-who-god-according-bible/

https://enduringword.com/bible-commentary/proverbs-1/

https://biblehub.com/commentaries/clarke/proverbs/2.htm

https://enduringword.com/bible-commentary/1-kings-3

https://www.brettmccracken.com/blog/2017/8/3/five-facets-of-our-epistemological-crisis.

https://enduringword.com/bible-commentary/proverbs-1/

https://enduringword.com/bible-commentary/proverbs-2/

https://enduringword.com/bible-commentary/proverbs-3/

/ 1 / UNDERSTANDING THE FOUNDATION OF WISDOM

/ 2 /

BEYOND HUMAN INTELLIGENCE: TAPPING INTO THE POWER OF SPIRITUAL INTELLIGENCE

I WILL ALLUDE to the story of Frederick Douglas, as it demonstrates a triumph of spirit (we are fundamentally spirit) over external circumstances. Born into slavery in 1818, he was soon separated from his mother before age one. His mother passed away soon after, and he only saw her four or five times. In his memoir Douglas confided that, "In the hottest summer and coldest winter, I was kept almost naked... I had no bed." Despite the adversity that characterized his early life, he defied all odds to become a powerful voice, inspired, motivated, and driven by more than human intellect. How? At some point in his life, the wife to his slave master taught Douglas the alphabet. On finding out, his slave master castigated and rebuked the wife.

Douglas's master told the wife not only was it illegal to teach a slave how to read, but he added, "It would forever unfit him to be a slave. He would at once become unmanageable, and of no value to his master." Additionally, the master stated that if there's one thing he should never read, it is the Bible.

After this ordeal, Frederick Douglas realized that his master—who had the power even to take his life and not be charged or convicted—was radically against his education or enlightenment of any kind. It was a watershed moment in the life of Frederick Douglas that resonated with something deeper within him. With determination, he went on to tap into something far deeper within his inner core—a spiritual intelligence that illuminated his path. His ability to overcome adversity and perceive the greater truth, resulting in wise living that defied his external circumstances, is testament to spiritual intelligence. This spiritual intelligence transcends human intelligence, it is the part of us that is divine and our true essence.

Like Douglas, we all face adversity that requires more than logic or intellect to overcome. Come with me on a journey to explore the power of spiritual intelligence that births wisdom to overcome physical limitations, leading to a life of contentment and fulfilment.

Often a time, *intelligence* and *wisdom* are used interchangeably. However, intelligence has to do more with knowing and retaining facts, whereas wisdom involves applying knowledge and understanding in daily living. As an example, an intelligent person knows that salt is a solute, however a wise person will not add salt to tea. Important to note is that intelligence is not tantamount to wisdom. However, there's a kind of intelligence that goes beyond academic, social, and emotional intelligence. It is called *spiritual intelligence* (superconscious).

To understand spiritual intelligence requires knowing and understanding that we are fundamentally spirit. How? In Genesis 1, God created mankind in his image and likeness, then in Genesis 2 he formed man from dust of the earth and breathed his Spirit into his nostrils. Specifically, Moses the Prophet corroborates that:

"The Lord God formed a man from the dust of the ground and breathed into his nostrils the breath of life, and the man became a living being."

—Genesis 2:7

On introducing the breath of life, which is the Spirit into the body, mankind became a living being (soul). This highlights a profound revelation that there's a part of us that is formed, and another that is created. We know that the body is formed through a biological process resulting in a gestation period of nine months. Out of our human experiences coupled with formal and informal education plus the environment, a sociological program that is your soul is formed. And spirit is the part of us that is created by God. Spirit man speaks to the divine essence of a male and female human being. It is the image and likeness of God in us which is the basis of our fundamental identity—we are fundamentally spirit. In the spirit, human beings are inducted into the God class.

Spirit is the part of God made from God characterized by Divine DNA. Since we are like God in spirit, then in essence we are inherently omnipotent, omnipresent, and omniscient.

We are all-knowing, all-powerful, and ubiquitous via thought. This a fundamental truth. Creativity, genius, great inventions, and innovations, deep spiritual experiences, great works of art, to name but a few, originate in spirit. Spirit is the seat of spiritual intelligence which is Godly wisdom. Our greatest calling is to discover the divine within us, and that part speaks to our ability to create just like God the Creator.

You see, in Genesis 1 God shows one important thing that is the essence of who He is, and that is the potential and power to create. Not only that, but recognizing that creation was by the Word of God—*Logos*, which is the reasoning power of God. Since we are created in the image and likeness of God, then our potential and power to create is what places us in the God class. To this day, no animal has ever created anything that I know of. Why? Because the Divine creative gene is only found in humans, the spiritual intelligence, so to speak.

Important to note is that thought, or reason precedes the words that are spoken. Implying that thoughts precede words, hence the Word of God in creation was preceded by thought. Thoughts are spiritual in nature and are the things expressed in the physical. Therefore what is *not seen*. That is, thoughts gives rise to the seen, the physical. Put another way, the invisible produces the visible.

Hebrews 11:3 put it this way:

"By faith we understand that the universe was framed at God's command, so that what is seen was not made out of what was visible."

—Hebrews 11:3

From this we infer that the invisible is the realty expressed in the physical. And as humans created in the image of God, we have inherent ability to transform things from the unseen. This is our supernatural ability to create and innovate on this earth. It is the spiritual intelligence or superconscious that is the wisdom of God within us. One may say that is purely religious stuff that can't be validated, but I will attempt to provide a scientific parallel.

In science we are told that anything that occupies space and has weight is matter. Matter is made up of molecules, and atoms make up molecules. This downward progression to the smallest asserts that atoms are made up of even smaller particles entailing neutrons, protons, and electrons. Now science also tells us that quarks are smaller particles than protons and neutrons. Protons are positively charged, while electrons are negatively charged, implying that they are energy. We can therefore deduce that matter originates from energy. Other than light that is the only form of energy visible to the human eye, as energy is invisible. So we can safely say that matter is made from things that are not seen, which parallels Hebrews 11:3 or John 1: 1-3.

"In the beginning was the Word, and the Word was with God, and the Word was God. He was with God in the beginning. Through him all things were made; without him nothing was made that has been made."

—John 1: 1-3

Furthermore, in theology God is described as omnipotent, omnipresent, eternal, and omniscient. In science, the law of conservation states that energy is neither created nor destroyed and it's forever taking on new forms. Hence energy is eternal and everlasting.

- And we just saw that energy comprises the smallest particles that make up matter, hence everything is *energy—omnipresent*. It follows that then that...

- different forms of energy like heat or nuclear energy demonstrate the power and might of *energy* — *omnipotent*.

- And since thoughts precede everything created, then thoughts are energy, and thoughts are reasoning *power* — *omniscient*.

Deductively, science and theology are two sides of the same coin. Hence, God is the Ultimate Energy or Ultimate Realty, and we are made in His image and likeness. You too have the essence of omnipotence, omnipresence, and omniscience. This is the immutable truth that the devil doesn't want you to know. You are divine, and here to express you divinity in the physical. Created in the image and likeness of God. Therefore, it's paramount to recognize that *who* you are is confirmed in *whose* you are:

- Because He is a Creator, you have the essence to create.

- Because He is a Ruler, you have the essence to rule.

- Because He is King, you are to be king of your assignment on earth.

For the Creator and Sovereign God says:

"Before I formed you in the womb I knew you, before you were born I set you apart; I appointed you as a prophet to the nations."

—Jeremiah 1:5

Or...

"Your eyes saw my unformed body; all the days ordained for me were written in your book before one of them came to be."

—Psalms 139:16

The implication from these verses is that you are complete and not lacking in anything before your conception. And this revelation about you is in the spirit, which is your spiritual intelligence. God already told you everything

He will ever say about you. This entails who you are, where you are from, purpose, potential, and destiny. Within you is everything you will ever need to express your desires, dreams, and goals.

When you believe this without a doubt, then you recognize that success is your birthright. It's the recognition that *eventually success is coming my way*. This is the fundamental truth about you.

Carl Sagan postulates:

"The truth may be puzzling. It may take some work to grapple with. It may be counterintuitive. It may contradict deeply held prejudices. It may not be consonant with what we desperately want to be true. But our preferences do not determine what's true."

—Carl Sagan

When we let go of *our truth*, then we discover *the Truth*. And the Truth about you is that you have original pre-conception intelligence—spiritual intelligence so to speak. That is the essence of who you are and whose you are.

The greatest paradox lies in surrendering our intelligence or intellect, which is the precursor to receiving God's wisdom—spiritual intelligence. It requires overcoming our delusions and illusions. I can safely say that nothing we hold in our mind is true. Why? Because we don't see things as they are, but rather from the perspective of who we are. Therefore tapping into our spiritual intelligence requires to reach that point of "I don't know," accepting and acknowledging one's deficiency or inadequacy—human limitation—then surrendering to God's truth.

When we let go of our truth, then and only then do we discover the Truth—that is, God's wisdom which is spiritual intelligence. In the words of Bryce Haymond, philosopher and writer:

"The radical realty may be that nothing that we think or hold in our mind is true. None of it. Not.

A. Word, Not. A. Single. Concept. At least they are not absolutely true. But that can be too much for the mind to handle, and so it creates all kinds of illusions to believe in, symbols to invest itself in, ideologies to hang its life on, religions that it claims are the absolute truth. But when any of those ideas or symbols or illusions fails, so to goes the mind."

—Bryce Haymond

"Failure of the mind" may seem to be a bad thing, but failure of the mind is key to its transformation, as then and only then do we surrender to the Wisdom of God.

At its core, spiritual intelligence is pre-conception supernatural wisdom that is forever flowing through us, seeking expression in the physical. Mind experts suggest that our mind consists of the superconscious, conscious, and subconscious dimensions:

- The conscious mind is the evidence of what we say,

- the subconscious mind is the evidence of our actions,

- and the superconscious is the divine energy forever flowing through us.

In his book, *You Were Born Rich*, Bob Proctor mentions that:

"In truth, you will never see the greatest part of your being because it is non-physical in nature. In fact, you will soon become aware that you are constantly living simultaneously on three distinct planes of being—you **ARE SPIRITUAL**, you **HAVE AN INTELLECT**, and you **LIVE IN A PHYSICAL BODY**."

— Bob Proctor, *You Were Born Rich*

This implies that you are living simultaneously in three dimensions or worlds:

1. The spiritual world of thought (highest potential);

2. The intellectual world of ideas (middle potential),

3. The physical world of results (lowest potential).

And *spirit* is our authenticity.

You must very well be asking, "How can I practically tap into the divine energy so as to express it in the physical world." Paul the Apostle answers:

"Do not conform to the pattern of this world, but be transformed by the renewing of your mind. Then you will be able to test and approve what God's will is—His good, pleasing, and perfect will."

—Romans 12:2

Transforming one's mindset is key. Divine energy is always flowing through us, but we have to be intentional so as to give it direction. Important to note is that whether we engage the divine energy or not, it still flows through us and will be expressed in the physical. So spiritual intelligence makes us aware of our ability to transport things from the invisible by directing the divine energy deliberately and express the desired outcome in the visible realm. This involves deliberate higher thoughts to be originated, causing a higher frequency of vibration. And the level of vibration determines what we express in the physical.

"Therefore, as soon as you choose certain thoughts, your brain cells are affected. These cells vibrate and send off electromagnetic waves. When you concentrate on those thoughts, you increase the amplitude of vibration of those cells, and the electrical waves, in turn, become much more potent."

—Bob Proctor

Hence, spiritual intelligence permits us to see beyond the superficial, transcend the ego-mind, and gain access into the deeper truth of any situation. We recognize that human wisdom is predicated on what is logical or practical, but spiritual wisdom honors God and righteousness.

Practically, we cultivate spiritual intelligence by:

- Recognizing, discerning, and operating from the "I am endowed with extraordinary mental superiority," perspective. Why? Because you are in the image and likeness of God. He already completed you in spirit and you already equipped with potential and ability live fulfilled and successful per God's will.

- Recognizing that in this world our struggle is not against 'flesh and blood' but spirits. As confirmed in the Bible; *"For our struggle is not against flesh and blood, but against the rulers, against the authorities, against the powers of this dark world and against the spiritual forces of evil in the heavenly realms.*" (Ephesians 6:12). Implying that we are against spiritual systems with human actors as the vehicles of spiritual activity. This is true in the political, economic, cultural, and spiritual systems.

- Regularly devote and commit to studying Scripture so as gain insight and revelation of God's plan and purpose for our life.

- Seek the direction of the Holy Spirit through prayer so as to make wise decisions in your daily life.

- Through prayer and reflection incline your inner ear to discernment of God's voice. Important to understand is that God speaks to you from within in a familiar voice which is your voice.

- And recognizing that the fundamental truth about mankind lies in his ability to originate thoughts he desires.

A compelling example of spiritual intelligence is evident in how we navigate relationships. Relationships—be it intimate, acquaintances, or work partnerships—will be fulfilling when premised on Godly wisdom that entails kindness, patience, love, or self-control. Where there's any form of human interaction, conflict is inevitable. However, Godly wisdom will lead us to recognize that forgiveness is to our benefit.

Why? When we forgive, we create a more conducive environment for everyone by letting go of any bitterness or resentment. We may feel it necessary to enact revenge, retaliate, or hold a grudge when hurt by others; however, spiritual intelligence establishes a deeper awareness of who we are based on *whose* we are. Implying we recognize, understand, and are aware of our co-existence with the Source, the One, the Ultimate Realty, the Sovereign God who is Truth, Love, Gracious, and Merciful. Since we are in His image and likeness, in relationships we are to extend grace, love, peace, and forgiveness to others.

Spiritual intelligence is an awareness that transcends the ego identity or the finite body-mind. It is a consciousness of connection and co-existence with the Divine Source, God, Creator, Ultimate Energy, Ultimate Realty or the One. This is the key to living a life subordinate to the authority and purpose of God. A life that is happiness, health, and wealth. Because of this awareness, you recognize that you co-exist with the infinite Source, and therefore you are limitless in your ability.

You understand what is within you determines what is expressed outside of you. Meaning that the invisible is the realty that gives meaning to the physical. You now understand that your thoughts maybe invisible, but it's them that will be expressed in the physical. That is, visible things originate from the invisible.

Therefore:

"Only by much searching and mining, are gold and diamonds obtained, and man can find every truth connected with his being, if he will dig deep into the mine of his soul; and that he is the maker of his character, the moulder of his life, and the builder of his destiny, he may unerringly prove, if he will watch, control, and alter his thoughts, tracing their effects upon himself, upon others and upon his life and circumstances, linking cause and effect by patient practice and investigation, and utilizing his every experience, as a means of obtaining the knowledge of himself which is Understanding, Wisdom, Power."

—James Allen.

References

As A Man Thinketh: A Book That Will Help You To Help Yourself byJames Allen.

You Were Born Rich: The Keys To Maximizing The Awesome Potential You Were Born With by Bob Proctor.

https://www.thymindoman.com/letting-go-of-our-truth-is-how-find-the-truth/

Narrative Of The Life Of Frederick Douglas by Frederick Douglas

https://chem.libretexts.org/bookshelves/introductory_chemistry/introduction_to_general_chemistry...

https://www.ananda.org/yogapedia/superconsciousness/

Spiritual Intelligence For Entrepreneurs by Bishop Wayne Malcolm.

/ 3 /

UNVEILING THE TRUE MEANING OF GOD'S WISDOM

LET ME BEGIN this chapter by making a bold statement:

No matter how high we rise, without God's wisdom guiding us, we are destined to fall short of true success and lasting fulfillment.

Intuitively, without God's wisdom, true success and fulfillment will forever elude mankind. This means that without divine direction, every worldly accomplishment is empty. I believe most of us are aware of a persistent void that lingers on until we submit our will to the authority of God. This shouldn't come as a surprise because God is Our Creator and we are His product, implying that the reason for our existence lies in Our Maker. So it is paramount that we align our plans with the purpose of the Creator in order to truly be successful and content.

A common practice from human manufacturers is the provision of a manual for every product they make. Why? Therein lies the mind of the human maker about the details guaranteeing successful operation of his product. In similar fashion, God Our Creator provided us ample detail in the Spirit-breathed Biblical Scripture. Herein lies the Word of God that is Divine wisdom guaranteeing us true success and fulfillment, on condition that we obey His commands.

Important to note is that God desires that we succeed, and He wants His Wisdom to be our own such that we reflect His glory—His nature, essence, and character. John the Apostle corroborates this profound idea:

"But when He, the Spirit of truth comes he will guide you into all the truth. He will not speak on his own; he will speak only what he hears, and he will tell you what is yet to come. He will glorify me because it is from me that he will receive what he will make known to you."

—John 16:13-14

This is good news for those who believe. Why? Because it implies that in every undertaking victory is guaranteed when we submit to the will of God. Even when you feel like it is not working, it is still working on you and for you. As a believer, you go into every situation whether be it business, relationships, or whatever it is, with the unfair advantage of the Sovereign God as your partner.

Charles Spurgeon postulates:

"WISDOM is man's true path-
that which enables him to
accomplish best the end of his
being, and which, therefore, gives
to him the richest enjoyment, and
the fullest play for all his powers.
Wisdom is the compass by which
man is to steer across the
trackless waste of life. Without
wisdom man is as the wild asses'
colt; he runs hither and thither,
wasting strength which might be
profitably employed."

Spurgeon goes on to say:

"Without wisdom, man may be
compared to a soil untilled,
which may yield some fair
flowers, but can never yield a
harvest which shall repay the
labor of the reaper, or even the
toil of the gleaner. Give man
wisdom, wisdom in the true

sense of the term, and he rises to
all the dignity that manhood can
possibly know; he becomes a fit
companion for the angels, and
between him and God there is no
creature; he standeth next to the
Eternal One, because Christ has
espoused his nature, and so has
linked humanity with divinity."

I couldn't have said it any better—someone
needs to be screaming and praising the Mighty
God, Wonderful Counselor, and Prince of
peace.

In the final verses of the book of Romans, the
Apostle Paul expresses his overwhelming
gratitude and awe through a doxology, a hymn
of praise to God. He emphasizes God's wisdom
as he closes his letter, acknowledging the power
of God to strengthen believers and the
revelation of the sacred secret kept silent for
ages, now made known through the prophetic
Scriptures. Paul's intention is to open a window
in the minds of his audience to the infinite
expanses of God, particularly focusing on God's
wisdom. He aims to help his audience see and

admire God's wisdom more intensely, leading to increased trust, obedience, and joy.

Let's focus on a powerful statement that will shape our perspective and transform our lives: God is infinitely wise. This truth carries profound implications that can bring comfort, alleviate anxiety, and inspire a deeper prayer life. According to the Bible, wisdom entails understanding the ultimate goal in any situation and determining the best course of action to achieve that goal (Sermon by John Piper, "The Great Work of the Only Wise God," based on Romans 16:25-27). It's important to note that wisdom goes beyond mere knowledge, as it involves integrating various sources of knowledge and experiences to make sound decisions.

Consider the following attribute and reflect on the nature of God. In this contemplation, heed the words of the psalmist who regarding God proclaims:

"His understanding is infinite"

—Psalm 147:5

Furthermore, take note of Jeremiah's invocation to the...

"great and mighty God whose name is the Lord of Hosts, the One great in counsel and mighty in deed, whose gaze encompasses the paths of humanity, rewarding each individual according to their ways and deeds"

—Jeremiah 32:19

In the same vein, Daniel, in his depiction of God's wisdom, records:

"He changes the times and
seasons; He removes kings and
establishes kings. He imparts
wisdom to the wise and
knowledge to those who have
understanding. He reveals the
deep and hidden things; He
knows what is in the darkness,
and light dwells with Him"

—Daniel 2:21-22

Notably, nothing remains enigmatic to God.
He is perpetually devoid of perplexity,
confusion, or uncertainty.

In the book of Romans (11:33-36), the apostle
Paul reflects on the profound wisdom of God,
expressing deep admiration for it. He portrays
God's judgments and ways as immeasurable
and inscrutable, beyond human understanding.
Paul underscores the idea that no one can offer
counsel to God, as His wisdom surpasses
human comprehension. This passage serves as a
poignant reminder of the boundless nature of
God's wisdom and the inherent purpose of all
things to glorify Him.

The wisdom of God is unfathomable and unchanging. According to Romans 11:36, everything originates from God, through God, and returns to God, emphasizing the perfection of God's actions. It is proposed that God continuously processes vast amounts of information, resulting in flawless and comprehensive knowledge of every relevant aspect in every situation. This enables God to make the best decisions effortlessly. While human understanding of God's wisdom is limited, the implications of His wisdom are profound and worthy of contemplation.

God's wisdom assures us that He will bring about the best possible outcomes for the greatest number of people in the most effective way and for the longest time. This means that whatever your current situation, God is intelligently orchestrating it to achieve something significant in you and through you. Consider embracing the belief that the challenging problems in your life were orchestrated for the best possible, longest-lasting results. Imagine if everything in your life was part of a wise plan. How would that transform your anxiety into confidence in God? Lloyd Stilley, an American Pastor postulates:

"But it's right here where we push back. 'I would love to believe that, Lloyd, but it doesn't add up in my life. You call what has happened to me the best possible circumstances for me right now?"

—Lloyd Stilley

Of importance is to understand that God's ways are not our ways, so we need to have faith and conviction in Him whether it makes sense to us or not. Let's us be reminded by the truth that we live in a fallen world, and our wisdom is shaped by our experiences, environment, and education in this kind of world. This kind of wisdom is premised on the finite body-mind or ego, which we have to transcend and surrender our mind to the truth of God. In this imperfect world tainted by the Fall of man, all of creation suffers the consequences of sin. Despite God's wisdom, His children are not always shielded from iniquity and disaster and wicked people are not always punished. However, God's ultimate justice will prevail, as stated in Galatians:

"Do not be deceived: God cannot
be mocked. A man reaps what he
sows."

—Galatians 6:7

When it's all said and done, God will get in
the end, everything He intended in the
beginning. And this what the good news of the
gospel is about.

God's wisdom is such that it is foolishness
to the world. Why? Consider God's execution of
the salvation and redemption plan for man. In
accordance with God's infinite wisdom, He
selected a path of salvation through Christ that
appears entirely irrational to human
understanding. No mortal would have
conceived of a scheme involving the brutal
slaying of the Son of God for the sake of sinners.
However, precisely at the moment when it
appeared most foolish, God's wisdom
prevailed. At the pinnacle of His apparent
vulnerability, God's power was unleashed.

1Corinthians 1:25, articulates:

"For the foolishness of God is wiser than human wisdom, and the weakness of God is stronger than human strength."

—1 Corinthians 1:25

We, as individuals, lack the depth of knowledge required to comprehend the reasons behind pain, suffering, injustice, and brutality in this sin-ridden world.

However, when we acknowledge our lack of wisdom, then with faith and conviction turn to the God of wisdom, only then can the wisdom of God be unveiled to us. James corroborates this truth:

"If any of you lacks wisdom, you should ask God who gives generously to all without finding fault, and it will be given to you. But when you ask, you must believe and not doubt because the one who doubts is like a wave of the sea, blown and tossed by the wind."

—James 1:5-6

Therefore, the best way forward is to align our plans with the purpose of God. Instead of planning our own things and asking God to bless them, it is better to submit and subordinate our plans to will of God. For who knows a product better than its maker?

"What we have received is not
the spirit of the world, but the
Spirit who is from God, so that
we may understand what God
has freely given us."

—1 Corinthians 2:12

Ladies and gentlemen, this unequivocally implies that you and I require communion with Spirit of God so as to discern the wisdom of God and benefit from it. Hence, a person lacking the Spirit of God will rebel against the things that originate from God to the point of being a mocker or scorner because those things can only be discerned by the Spirit of God.

"Whence then cometh wisdom?
and where is the place of
understanding? Seeing it is hid
from the eyes of all living, and
kept close from the fowls of the
air. Destruction and death say,
we have heard the fame thereof
with our ears. God understandeth

the way thereof, and he knoweth,
and he knoweth the place
thereof."

—Charles Spurgeon.

References

https://www.spurgeon.org/resource-library/sermons/trust-in-god-true-wisdom/#flipbook/

https://www.lifeway.com/en/articles/sermon-wisdom-god-romans-16-1-corinthians-1

/ 4 /

WISDOM IS THE KEY THAT UNLOCKS THE DOOR TO TRUE LASTING WEALTH

WHAT IF EVERYTHING you have been chasing—that is, money, power, fame, and social status—was a distraction from discovering true wealth premised on wisdom? In attempting to answer this question, I will call attention to a short story about a rich man who paid a visit to a sage. It is said that the rich man was unhappy and troubled despite his material wealth. On hearing his dilemma, the sage directed the rich man to juggle three balls; a ceramic one, a glass one, and a rubber ball. Being a good student or desperate for an answer, the rich man proceeded as instructed. No sooner had he started juggling the three balls than he lost coordination and was about to drop the ceramic ball. Instead, he let the rubber ball fall to the ground while saving the ceramic ball.

After this, the sage inquired; "Why did you do that?"

"Because the ceramic ball would have broken," the rich man said.

The sage informed the rich man that the three balls represented priorities in life. Loved ones were represented by the ceramic ball, while necessities such has shelter, food, and job were represented by the glass ball, and the rubber ball symbolized luxuries. Thus far, the man always let the ceramic ball drop to the ground while saving the rubber ball. A case of misplaced priorities, and the reason for his unhappiness. The moral of this story is to value

people instead of things. In the pseudo-
economy, people tend to value things above
humans. From antiquity to now, the practice of
devaluing human beings at the expense of
things (luxuries) is commonplace. This is
repugnant and odious.

Accumulation of things shouldn't be an end
in itself, and this was the rich man's problem.
We live in a world dominated by a pseudo-
narrative when it comes to success. Materialism
or the love of stuff is a universal problem that
misrepresents the true meaning of wealth. Let
me digress a bit; there's nothing wrong with
desiring good stuff and going after it. However,
to pursue riches without a God-ordained
purpose is meaningless. The atheist believes
diligence is the precursor to wealth, the lazy
person desires wealth without the diligence for
it; however, a godly person attributes his source
of wealth to God, and backs it up with inspired
action.

In each of us God placed seed potential that
is in alignment to the big picture of God's will
for our life. Our task is to go to the God of
wisdom, ask for wisdom to discern His will for
our life. This places one at an advantage of
doing what God has already blessed. The

greatest mistake is for mankind to embark on executing plans that are outside God's will, and then asking God to bless them. Good success and prosperity are only possible by aligning our plans with that which is already blessed by God. True wealth arises from recognizing one's original reason for existence. Why? Because it is already blessed by God and it aligns with God's purpose for our lives.

To successfully fulfill one's original reason for existence calls for divine guidance through the Spirit of God. For who knows the thoughts of God other than His Spirit? In similar fashion man's thoughts are known by his spirit.

"For who knows a person's thoughts except their own spirit within them? In the same way no one knows the thoughts of God except the Spirit of God."

—Corinthians 2:11

And when there's communion between the Spirit of God, and man's spirit, illumination of man by God's wisdom takes place. In essence

God is wisdom; however, His wisdom manifests through human beings via their choices, actions, and decisions. By faith we understand that the worlds were framed by the Word of God, such that the visible things didn't come from things that are seen.

"By faith we understand that the universe was formed at God's command, so that what is seen was not made out of what was visible."

—Hebrews 11:3

This implies that since we were created in the image and likeness of God, then we have the essence of God in us, and by words we bring about the circumstances that define our life. Words are not just words; they are also the lens through which we see our world. A wise person recognizes this truth, then deliberately and intentionally originates thoughts that align with their inherent desires. Thinking involves words we say, so it's important to pay attention to our thoughts. Why?

Because thoughts become ideas, and ideas translate into imaginations, imaginations become plans, plans that become the basis for action. God gives us ideas that translate into opportunities; however, only with wisdom can we generate outcomes from these opportunities. This truth is corroborated by Thomas Troward:

"If people only realized the truth that 'good' is not a certain limited quantity, but a stream continuously flowing from the exhaustless Infinite, and ready to take any direction we choose to give it, and that each one is able by the action of his own thoughts to draw from it indefinitely."

—Thomas Troward

The implication is that abundance from the Source, the One, the Ultimate Realty is exhaustless, but a spiritual conscious awareness of this truth is necessary. The idea that resources are limited and scarce is one of the greatest lies from the great liar, the devil. The devil utilizes deception to get people to focus

on what they think is lacking in any situation.
Let me allude to the garden of Eden narrative to
clearly illustrate this matter.

After creating man, God placed him in the
Garden of Eden with clear instruction to eat
freely from any tree other than the one that was
in the midst of the garden. Then the devil
appeared to mankind and asked:

"Did God really say, you must
not eat from any tree in the
garden?"

—Genesis 3:1

Clearly, we see that the devil took God's
Word out of context and shifted the
conversation from the tree to God's essence.
After a back and forth conversation between the
devil and mankind, man abandoned God's
instructions and embraced the devil's
suggestions. This implied that man chose to
side with a lie instead of the Truth of God. This
implied that man shifted his focus from
abundance to scarcity in a mental sense. You
have to realize that where there's conversation

the mind is involved, that is the conscious and subconscious mind implying conscious awareness.

In embracing the lies of the devil, man's mental programming took on a negative perspective (scarcity and limitation), implying man abandoned his original mental programming which is the Creative Success Mechanism (infinite conscious awareness of co-existence with a limitless Source) that is under the guidance of the Spirit of God. You see, man is fundamentally spirit as well as astral in nature. In spirit, man is aware of his limitless ability because he/she co-exists with the Infinite One. In spirit man has a conscious awareness that transcends the finite physical body.

I will allude to the law of polarity so as to clearly expound the relationship between spiritual and physical. The law of polarity is a universal principle that states "Everything has an opposite on the same continuum." Where there is a decrease, there is also an increase; where there is light, there is darkness; where there is cold, there is heat; where there is good, there is bad; where there is physical laws, there is spiritual laws, ad infinitum. To everything there is the opposite. Each cannot exist without the other. Existence itself cannot exist without the opposites.

Living out these polarities is part and parcel of the human experience. Therefore, spirit and body are two sides of the same coin where the spirit seeks expression in the physical. And the truth about you and me is that Infinite Spirit is forever flowing through us seeking expression.

This is affirmed by Bob Proctor:

"Spirit never expresses itself other than perfectly. And Spirit is always for expansion and fuller expression. If you let the higher side of your nature naturally unfold, your relationships will get better, you'll have more money, you'll feel better... and everything in your life will improve."

—Bob Proctor

Wisdom is the discernment of this truth, such that we are able to identify what we don't want, and become more aware of what we desire. This reminds me of the famous question that Christ Jesus, asked His archenemies:

"You foolish people! Did not the one who made the outside make the inside also?"

—Luke 11:40

Jesus Christ was irritated and disturbed by the tendencies of the Pharisees (religious representation instead of Kingdom of God). They always focused on outside circumstances and conforming to those circumstances. Meaning that their thinking was from the outside in. Instead, Christ wanted them to realize that the proper order of thinking should be from the inside out. Doing this ensures that one's higher nature that is spirit dictates what the outside circumstances look like, implying that abundance from within will always be expressed on the outside. This is what guarantees lasting wealth.

Important to note is that wealth is two dimensional in nature; spiritual and material.

But the truth is that material wealth is an expression of spiritual essence; therefore, spirit gives meaning to material. Spiritual is higher thought and energetic vibrations so to speak. When you align yourself with higher vibrations, your desired outcomes become realty. Recognizing this truth is wisdom that translates into wealth. This wisdom starts with awareness of the inherent capacity such that one recognizes their ability to turn what they have into what they need or desire.

For this to happen, one has to abandon fear, worry, and anxiety and embrace faith and conviction in the Creator.

In his book *Psycho-Cybernetics*, Maxwell Maltz asserts:

"We could relieve ourselves of a vast load of care, anxiety, and worry if we could but recognize the simple truth that our Creator made ample provisions for us to live successfully in this or any other age by providing us with a built-in Creative Mechanism."

— Maxwell Maltz, *Psycho-Cybernetics*

Jesus Christ once said:

"Take no thought for tomorrow."

—Mathew 6:34

This same message was reiterated by Paul the Apostle:

"Be careful in nothing."

—Philippians 4:6

Implying that fear, worry, and anxiety works against the inherent success mechanism that is in each of us. It's advised that we surrender and let go of worry, then through faith we are able to activate the creative success mechanism to work in our favor. It is called victory by surrender:

"Give up the feeling of responsibility, let go your hold, resign the case of your destiny to higher powers, be genuinely indifferent as to what becomes of it all... It is but giving your private convulsive self a rest, and finding that a greater Self is there. The results slow or sudden, or great or small, of the combined optimism and expectancy, the regenerative phenomena which ensure on the abandonment of effort, remain firm facts of human nature."

—Maxwell Maltz

Recognizing the higher Self in you is key to tapping into the power and mechanism that guarantees success. Realizing that you have the ability to set a clearly defined goal, which becomes the basis for your actions and behaviors. And this ability is premised on the fact that there's One greater at work within you. Because of His limitless ability, you have the ability to convert desires into realty. This is wisdom.

Furthermore, recognizing that each one of us has a gift or talent unique to them is paramount in building wealth that lasts. Often a time, people tend to focus on what they think they lack and lose insight about what lies within them. Wisdom is the understanding that no matter what the outside circumstances are, I have something within me to produce desired outcomes on the outside. This idea parallels an excerpt from the parable of ten minas:

"He replied, I tell you that to everyone who has, more will be given, but as for the one who has nothing, even what they have will be taken away."

—Luke 19:20

The takeaway from this is twofold: first when one becomes aware of the truth that they have inherent gifts, talents, unique experiences, or skills then harnessing them results in abundance. Secondly, it's clear each one of us has some inherent gifting or something at our disposal because this statement from Luke above; "but as for the one who has nothing, even what they have will be taken away," confirms this truth. Each one of us has something, and wisdom is the awareness of that something in nothing.

Additionally, of importance is the insight to acknowledge the existence of latent power in what we have. Therefore, wisdom is about being conscious of the dormant power within that something in us or that something unique to us. Activation of this potential produces the desired outcomes. Consider the story of the widow and Elisha, the prophet. She was heavily indebted such that failure to pay would tantamount to losing her two sons to her creditors. So she approached Elisha the prophet for a bail out. The man of God asked her if she owned anything of value, and the response was "only a pot of oil (2 Kings 4:1-2)." Like many of us, we tend to overlook the potential power present at our disposal. However, wisdom lies in recognition of this latent power in what we already have. This dormant ability is the seed potential present in each of us, otherwise God wouldn't have commanded us to be fruitful in the first place.

When God calls us to be fruitful (Genesis 1:26-27), it implies the seed is already present. Because, whatever God calls for, He provides. Therefore, the key to dominion lies in recognition and harnessing of the seed potential within us. Activating dormant ability or latent power or seed potential is only possible with the understanding that seeds don't look like the fruits they produce. Also, insight and recognition to the fact that keys don't resemble the doors they open. Opportunity is more often than not disguised in a suit called opposition.

Where opportunity dwells, there also is adversity.

Wisdom informs us that every good intention is almost always followed by a disruption. However, Spirit is always moving, and our task is to remain in touch with Spirit and be in-spirit resulting in inspiration. Inspiration will be followed by knowledge and understanding. Therefore wisdom informs one that potential within is the key to the abundance one desires, irrespective of the outside circumstances. Wisdom informs us that the little at our disposal is the key to the abundance that we desire. Therefore, abundance, prosperity, and good success arise out of recognizing the untapped potential power within each of us.

Now, nurturing the seed potential is the cornerstone of enjoying lasting wealth. It calls for a fertile environment of the spirit and soul that is watered and nourished by the truth of the Word of God which is wisdom. Important to note is that God created mankind and then placed them in the Garden of Eden, not a pantry. Why a garden? Because in the garden which symbolizes God's economy, consumption implies more productivity.

Understanding this truth is key to gaining and enjoying wealth that lasts. Consumption of fruit and disposing off seed results in growth of more plants or trees that bear more fruit. Only God can tell the number of fruits in a seed, that is why submitting to His will is key to living a life of abundancy and wealth without sorrow. Man on his own can accumulate wealth, but it will come with care, anxiety and worry.

The better way is for mankind to water and nourish the soils of the hearts, such that the seed of the Word of God can take root in our hearts. How we do this is by receiving the Truth of God without a doubt. Only God gives us the power to make wealth, and this is corroborated in Deuteronomy:

"And you shall remember the LORD your God, for it is He who gives you power to get wealth, that He may establish His covenant which He swore to your fathers, as it is this day."

—Deuteronomy 8:18

The takeaway from this verse is threefold: firstly, as humans we tend to seek God's blessings in times of great need, but quick to forget Him in times abundance. We have to always remember that God is the Ultimate Source of true and lasting wealth. Secondly, normally mankind focuses on diligence and their own intellect as the power to gain wealth. But the truth is that God gives the brain, the body, and the talent. Therefore, wisdom lies in understanding it is He who gives you power to get wealth. Thirdly, wisdom informs us that God gives us wealth to further His eternal purpose. It is unwise to use your material blessing to serve selfish ends. Of importance is to use material success for purposes of advancing God's Kingdom.

King Solomon considered to be the wisest and richest man in Scripture, ranked wisdom above everything else. When asked by God to ask for anything he desires, he chose wisdom to govern justly instead of power, fame, and fortune. This pleased God, that he granted Solomon wisdom beyond measure in addition to unmatched wealth and prosperity. As we see in Kings:

"At Gibeon the Lord appeared to Solomon during the night in a dream, and God said, 'Ask for whatever you want me to give you.'

"Solomon answered, 'You have shown great kindness to your servant, my father David, because he was faithful to you and righteous and upright in heart. You have continued this great kindness to him and have given him a son to sit on his throne this very day.

"'Now, Lord my God, you have made your servant king in place of my father David. But I am only a little child and do not know how to carry out my duties. Your servant is here among the people you have chosen, a great people, too numerous to count or number. So give your servant a discerning heart to govern your people and to distinguish between right and wrong. For

who is able to govern this great
people of yours?'

"The Lord was pleased that
Solomon had asked for this. So
God said to him, 'Since you have
asked for this and not for long
life or wealth for yourself, nor
have asked for the death of your
enemies but for discernment in
administering justice, I will do
what you have asked. I will give
you a wise and discerning heart,
so that there will never have been
anyone like you, nor will there
ever be. Moreover, I will give you
what you have not asked for—
both wealth and honor—so that
in your lifetime you will have no
equal among kings. And if you
walk in obedience to me and keep
my decrees and commands as
David your father did, I will give
you a long life.'"

—1 Kings 3:5-14

The wisdom of Solomon attracted him greater influence and honor than wealth or power alone could ever have garnered. Corroborating that true and lasting wealth emanates from understanding, discernment, and aligning one's heart with God's agenda.

Warren Buffet is considered by many as one of the wealthiest people on earth in the modern world. Well known for his success in business and investment, Buffet has repeatedly postulated that lifelong learning, strategic thinking, and a commitment to his principles are the mantra to his success. A combination of knowledge, deliberate and intentional decision-making geared toward long-term investing, rather than fame, power or short-term gains are the principles behind Buffet's success. His track record demonstrates a man who is content, influential and financially secure. Which is a result of consistent wise decision making over a long period of time. In both examples, the common denominator is wisdom as the foundation upon which true and lasting wealth is built.

When it's all said and done, wisdom is the master key that opens the door to lasting wealth and contentment. Why? Because fame, fortune and power guarantee fleeting success, but not contentment. Wisdom opens our eyes of understanding thereby equipping us with the vision, diligence, and composure to overcome the tempests of life. By seeking, searching, and gaining wisdom we discover that authentic wealth is not a factor of accumulation of material, but the values and principles we uphold, how we live, and the legacy that goes beyond us. Wisdom guarantees a life of purpose. abundance, and lasting peace:

"Therefore whosoever heareth these sayings of mine, and doeth them, I will liken him unto a wise man which built his house upon a rock: and the rain descended, and the floods came, and the winds blew and beat upon that house, and it fell not: for it was founded upon a rock."

—Mathew 7:24-25

Implying that wisdom is the bedrock upon which true and lasting wealth is built.

In the end, wisdom is the knowledge and understanding that in the Kingdom of God's economy abundance and not scarcity is the norm. The devil still employs the same method of deception that orients people to focus on lack rather than abundance; just like he did to Adam and Eve. However, those who believe in their hearts and confess with their mouths that Christ is Lord, become new individuals with awareness of the abundance that abounds in God's Kingdom. Faith and conviction in God elevates one's spirit to the awareness that success and fulfillment is inevitable. Wisdom is premised on the recognition of the truth that when you align your plans with the purpose of God, then you are operating under what is already blessed by God. Nothing compares to living and working under what God has already blessed. For this is more precious and of more value than silver, gold, and rubies.

"Choose my instruction instead
of silver, knowledge rather than
choice gold, for wisdom is more
precious than rubies, and nothing
you desire can compare with
her."

—Proverbs 8: 10-11

Where there's lack of wisdom, one may have
riches of this world but miserable.

References

The Hidden Power And Other Papers Upon Mental Science by Thomas Troward.

https://beaninspirer.medium.com/short-stories-that-are-source-of-knowledge-and-moral-values-1f1fa1a845cc

12 Laws of The Universe by Manhardeep Singh.

Psycho-Cybernetics by Maxwell Maltz, MD, FICS.

You Were Born Rich by Bob Proctor.

https://enduringword.com/bible-commentary/deuteronomy-8/

/ 5 /

KINGDOM FIRST, THEN LASTING WEALTH

THERE'S NO KINGDOM on earth that is an authentic reflection of the Kingdom of God. Why? Because the Kingdom of God is a spiritual realm of ultimate realty, ultimate truth, ultimate wisdom, wealth, purpose, love, and justice that transcends what any human nation can ever achieve. However, for clarity I will attempt to expound what it means to be a kingdom citizen by using an earthly kingdom as an example. After which I will delve deeper into the Kingdom of God.

Qatar is a Kingdom or hereditary monarchy with one of the largest reserves of petroleum and natural gas. Due to the immense oil and natural gas wealth, the citizens of Qatar are some of the luckiest people on earth. This is because Qatari citizenship guarantees perks that are substantial in nature. As a Qatari, one is born into a system that ensures tax-free income, high-paying government jobs, free education, free healthcare, subsidized electric and water bills. The government goes as far as providing financial support for newlyweds, and housing support. In addition the government spends heavily on military which makes it one of the safer countries to live in. Therefore, for a Qatari citizen abundance, protection, and provision from government is a birthright. Loyalty to the Emir is paramount.

No matter how great an earthly kingdom (nation) may be, it is *pseudo* in nature. Why? Because earthly kingdoms always subjugate their people. There is a royal family and subjects, and this goes against God's intended purpose. God created mankind for dominion over non-human creatures. So any attempt for man to rule over another human being is ungodly. God's intention for mankind is to govern His creation and creatures in a godly way. Wisdom entails understanding God's mandate for man that can only be executed under the Kingdom of God mandate. Unlike earthly kingdoms, the Kingdom of God only has one class of people. Everyone in God's Kingdom is royalty; therefore, the Kingdom of God is a Kingdom of kings. How is this arrangement possible, you may ask? Because every citizen in the Kingdom of God has an area of gifting that is their domain to rule.

Because there cannot be a kingdom without a king, in God's government we have a King of kings which is a *Kingdom of kingdoms*. Implying that each citizen in God's Kingdom has an area of gifting or talent that is their intended domain or kingdom to rule over. Wisdom lies in understanding that we are called to excel in our area of gifting so that we become of service to others. Dominion in a godly way is about becoming a slave to your gift and then serving it to others. This is what *kingdom rulership* in God's government means. It's the recognition that in each of us is a gift(s) that only we can develop to be of benefit to others. Implying that as what I am here to do is unique to me, only I can dedicate time and effort to bring it to fruition so as to benefit others and vice versa.

When we all do this, there's no need to compete with one another. Instead, we become makers and innovators that are rewarded for the value we create. This results in fulfillment and contentment due to doing the work that we were created to do. Wisdom is paramount when it comes to unlocking the mystery of the Kingdom of God. Yes there is a mystery in relation to the truth of the Kingdom of God, which can be understood by the intended audience. Wisdom is key in gaining knowledge, understanding, and then living out the Kingdom principles.

"Because it has been given to you to know the mysteries of the kingdom of heaven, but not to them it has not been given."

—Mathew 13:11

Clearly, this verse indicates there are those who don't understand the secrets of the kingdom. Either because they lack diligence, or they are blinded by their biases. On the other hand those who diligently seek and search for the kingdom are the intended audience. Therefore, the responsibility to decipher the concealed truth lies squarely on the individual. Understanding the spiritual truth of the kingdom mystery, and applying it is *wisdom*. This is wisdom that will benefit those who are spiritually sensitive.

When the seed of the Word of God takes root in the soils of our heart, we become ambassadors of the Kingdom. As Kingdom of God ambassadors we epitomize values, beliefs, and norms that reflect the essence of the Sovereign God. Our task should be about taking territory in the secular systems, and becoming key people of influence in those secular systems. This is achieved not through conquest but through influencing others by excelling in our areas of gifting. By wisdom we produce value, multiply, replenish, subdue, and have dominion. Dominating our areas of gifting is by creating value that results in contributing to others. Contribution results in cooperation that establishes connections.

Creativity, contribution, cooperation, and connection is commensurate with wealth.

Prioritization of the Kingdom is the master key to a life of fulfillment. When we give priority to seeking and searching for the Kingdom, wisdom becomes the map that leads to lasting prosperity. So how do we prioritize the Kingdom of God? Through submitting our plans to the authority of God. Doing this implies that God is the King who reigns in our hearts, such that He makes you to reign over your area of gifting. One thing to always remember is that our task is to please God and serve people.

This is done by serving through creativity. Right from the beginning we see God as a Creator, which is a clue to who we are since we are created in Hs image and likeness. Once God created mankind, He placed man in the garden to dress it and keep it.

"The Lord God took the man and put him in the Garden of Eden to work it and take care of it."

—Genesis 2:15

You see, everything in the garden was good, so our task was and is to make it better. Wisdom is the recognition that creativity through resourcefulness is the key to dominion. Each one of us was created to be an answer to a specific question, to be a solution to a problem, and to be the bridge to a gap in the life of others.

Essentially, wealth creation and fulfillment is only possible through focusing on coming up with a solution to someone else's problem. Doing this translates into others rewarding you for the service or product you create that fixes their problem. Make no mistake of focusing on the fulfillment of self-serving ends, instead concentrating on fulfilling other people's problems resulting into building wealth that lasts. As humans we tend to obsess with fulfilling our own ends, and in the process we are consumed by the never-ending chase of material desires. However, Scripture cautions us to not fret over material stuff:

"Therefore I say to you, do not worry about your life, what you will eat or what you will drink; nor about your body, what you will put on. Is not life more than food and the body more than clothing? Look at the birds of the air, for they neither sow nor reap nor gather into barns; yet your heavenly Father feeds them. Are you not of more value than they? Which of you by worrying can add one cubit to his stature?"

—Mathew 6: 25-27

When you focus on food and drink, it implies that your mind is serving the body which goes against the order of God. In the Kingdom of God your body should serve the mind and then your mind serves the spirit. So focusing on the fulfillment of material ends (food, drink, and clothes) to the point of fretting about them is ungodly. Why? Because the material stuff becomes your master, and your priority is out of order. It's the equivalent of serving Mammon—the false god of prosperity.

Wisdom brings to your attention the need to serve God. That is putting your faith and trust in God, and focus on being you just like the birds of the air or the lilies of the field. Birds are not trying to be fish or dogs or trees, they are focused on being birds. Implying that your attention, time, and effort should be directed on being and becoming the person God created you to be. No need trying to be like someone else. Yes you can draw inspiration from others; however, you shouldn't be competing against anyone. If you are going to compete, then your competition should be about becoming better than the person you were yesterday. Every waking hour, your task is to outdo today, the "yesterday you." And this is through a service premised on creativity in your area of gifting.

Remember to store your treasures in heaven and not on earth where the so-called treasures or symbols of success are fleeting in nature. Scripture corroborates this truth:

"Lay not up for yourselves treasures upon earth, where moth and rust doth corrupt, and where thieves break through and steal. But lay up for yourselves treasures in heaven, where neither moth nor rust doth corrupt, and where thieves do not break through nor steal: For

where your treasure is, there will
your heart be also."

—Mathew 6: 19-21

The implication is that earthly riches are
temporary and fleeting. Now, let me say this it
is not wrong to own material riches, but wisdom
should make you aware that they lack lasting
value. It is wrong to amass material riches for
self-aggrandizement as it demonstrates loyalty
to a false god. Instead, use earthly wealth to
advance the work of the Kingdom of God.
Leading to a sense of contentment and peace
due to being a giver to worthy causes. And the
work God does through us via faithful giving
lasts for eternity. Always remember that your
heart and treasure can only be in one place. And
if you choose to align your plans with the
throne of God, then purpose, provision, and
protection are guaranteed. No need to worry!

Your modus operandi should be to approach
life with singleness of purpose. Dedicating
yourself to accomplishing goals without
compromising your values. Wisdom informs
you that in the Kingdom of God's economy,
fulfillment is about accomplishing goals

without compromising your values. Values, and beliefs are a central part of your self-identity. Self-identity defines the boundaries of your thoughts, choices, and decision making.

How we see ourselves determines how we act and behave. Intuitively, fundamental identity determines one's awareness of the spiritual principles or kingdom keys. And I will boldly state that the greatest challenge facing man since the dawn of time is the issue of identity. People just simply don't know who they are in the deepest sense (image and likeness of God). And this brings to mind one of the greatest questions that Jesus Christ paused to his disciples:

"When Jesus came into the region of Caesarea Phillippi, He asked His disciples, saying, who do men say that I the Son of Man, am? So they said, some say John the Baptist, some Elijah, and others Jeremiah or one of the prophets. He said to them, but who do you say that I am? Simon Peter answered and said, you are

the Christ the Son of the living
God."

—Mathew 16: 13-16

Jesus asked this question not because he
didn't know who He was, but He was bringing
to our attention a very important principle, that
only the Creator can reveal to you who you are.
His response to Peter's answer was that Peter
didn't know this via his own knowledge, but
God revealed it to him. And went on to tell
Simon son of Jonah, that from now on you are
Peter, and upon that statement ("You are the
Christ, the Son of the living God.") I will build
my government.

I am saying all this, to bring to your
attention that when you get to know who God
is in the true sense of the matter, then He will
reveal to you who you are. Only and only this
will give you access to the keys of the kingdom.
Scripture corroborates this:

"And I will give you the keys of
the kingdom of heaven, and
whatever you bind on earth shall

have been bound in heaven, and
whatever you loose on earth shall
have been loosed in heaven."

—Mathew 16:19

The kingdom of heaven is the realm where
God rules, and earth is man's domain to rule.

Keys allude to and imply authority, power,
ownership, and access. Knowledge and
understanding informs that no spiritual entity
can interfere in earthly affairs without the
consent of mankind. Even God won't interfere
in our life, our circumstances, unless we invite
Him. This is also true for the devil. As humans
we have the responsibility to dominate earth.
And you as an individual, you were called for a
time such as this to dominate through creativity
and be of service to others. God is the Landlord,
and mankind is the tenant. The tenant is
responsible for management without the
interference of the landlord until the lease
expires.

When does it expire? In the end times.
Mankind can accomplish plenty without God;
however, fulfillment is impossible without God.
For now, you are to rule on behalf of the Lord

of lords. Your time is now, and now is all you have.

"But seek first the kingdom of God and His righteousness, and all these things shall be added to you."

—Mathew 6:33

For seeking first the Kingdom of God is the seed from which the tree of wisdom sprouts to bear abundant fruit.

References

https://medium.com/@thereallimit.com/facts-about-qatar-citizens-and-residents-7ed99f117660

/ 6 /

WISDOM IS THE TREE THAT YIELDS ABUNDANT FRUIT

WE ARE NOTIFIED in Scripture that God planted a garden eastward in Eden in which he placed the man He had formed. (Genesis 2:8). Now, there were three kinds of trees in the garden; trees good for food, the tree of knowledge of good and evil, and the tree of life. Man was able to gain access (with or without permission) to all the trees, except the tree of life, or is it? Proverbs 3:18 states:

"She is a tree of life to those who take hold of her, and happy are all who retain her."

—Proverbs 3:18

Here 'She' refers to wisdom; intuitively wisdom is a tree of life. And Christ Jesus asserted:

"The thief does not come except to steal, and to kill, and to destroy. I have come that they may have life, and that they may have it more abundantly."

—John 10:10

Hence, the life in the wisdom tree is one characterized by abundance. As believers, when we allow the seed of the Word of God take root in our hearts, the tree of wisdom springs forth and bears abundant fruit for us.

In one of the parables in Mathew 13, Jesus likened the Kingdom of God to a farmer who went out to sow seed, and this seed was the Word of God to various hearers. And clearly, mankind's priority is to seek first the Kingdom of God, and all the other material stuff will be drawn to them. Now, I am saying all that to say this that when attention, time, and effort is directed towards watering the seed of the wisdom tree, abundant fruit is the outcome.

Before the seed can produce fruit, it starts off by growing downward into the ground by a process called *gravitropism*. During gravitropism, roots are developed away from sunlight. And for the tree of wisdom in our hearts, roots entail our internal state. This state includes:

- beliefs

- values

- understanding

- knowledge

- perceptions

- imagination

- self-image

- mental programming

- and attitude.

Developing roots takes time, and it entails preparation and planning on our part. We have to cultivate values, beliefs, attitudes, skills, knowledge, perceptions, and a sense of self that aligns with our *prophetic purpose*. By prophetic purpose, I mean that we have to identify and see ourselves the way God see us such that we can fulfill our God-ordained purpose.

Let me digress for a minute, if you are Abram and fatherless God calls you out and says:

"Blessing I will bless you, and multiplying I will multiply your descendants as the stars of the heaven and as the sand which is on the seashore; and your descendants shall possess the gate of their enemies."

—Genesis 22:17

From this verse, you realize that God identifies you with your prophetic purpose. It doesn't matter what your current circumstances depict, don't make the mistake of identifying yourself with external circumstances. Abram was childless and old, but God called him Abraham implying the exalted father. Of importance is to always remember that developing roots happens in the dark, amidst trials, and takes time. However, even in the dark the Spirit of God is always on the move and will bring about inspiration, followed by light. (Genesis 1:2-3).

Therefore inspiration and illumination lead to phototropism, which is the upward growth towards light. With a formidable root system in

117

place, the wisdom tree develops a trunk and branches that will bear abundant fruit. The root system, trunk, and branches of the wisdom tree equals one's mindset, uniqueness, and skillset. These three are internal. These three determine the toolset one will employ in producing the desired outcomes. Outcomes are external.

Important to note is that the root system determines the fruit, or put another way one's internal state determines one's external circumstances. The desired outcome is the fruit of the wisdom tree. And in the Book of Proverbs the fruits of the wisdom tree are specified:

> "Happy is the man who finds wisdom, and the man who gains understanding; for her proceeds are better than profits of silver, and her gain than fine gold. She is more precious than rubies, and all the things you may desire cannot compare with her. Length of days is in her right hand, in her left hand riches and honor. Her ways are ways of pleasantness. And all her paths are peace. She is a tree of life to

those who take hold of her, and
happy are all who retain her."

—Proverbs 3: 13-18

Clearly, we can see that wise people not only accomplish material gains beyond compare, but also emotional and psychological benefits in the form of peace and joy.

And also; "alluding most manifestly to the tree so called which God in the beginning planted in the garden of Paradise, by eating the fruit of which all the wastes of nature might have been continually repaired, so as to prevent death." (Clarke). The root system of the wisdom tree parallels the kingdom within. Luke the Greek Physician put it this way:

"Nor will they say, see here or
see there, for indeed the kingdom
of God is within you."

—Luke 17:21

The kingdom within refers to one's internal world that is the source of the external world.

It's incumbent upon each of us to create an inner atmosphere that will produce the outcomes we desire. This responsibility is the mandate of every believer. You see there's a lot of external circumstances that are outside our control. For instance, the taxes imposed by governments, the prices of commodities, the opinions of others, these and many more. Wise people recognize that they are solely responsible for designing their internal state. As a wise person, you are the writer, director, and producer of your internal atmosphere.

Many people tend to focus on chasing external outcomes like jobs, houses, cars, and or millions of dollars; however, the fact is that these will conform towards the direction of one's internal world. For instance, a person may chance upon a windfall of say $5,000,000, but they have a $50,000 mentality. In no time they will be back to their old ways. Lottery winners that go bankrupt are a great example. Sharon Tirabassi cashed a $10 million Canadian dollars check in 2004. She was a single mother dependent on government welfare. In under ten years after winning the lottery she was back to riding the bus, working part-time, and staying in a rented house. She had squandered her fortune on a big house, fancy cars, designer clothes, parties, lavish trips, ad infinitum. Sharon's story shows that when the external circumstances are not congruent with the internal state of an individual, success is not sustainable.

Wisdom informs us that there's a correlation between one's internal world and external world. God's order of success is premised on the fact that the inside originates and determines the outside world. Is it not who made the outside, also made the inside? (Luke 11:40).

The Divine order follows the sequence of; be, do, and have which is premised on the foundation of time, space and matter. God's design from Genesis 1:28, requires one to first become the person that aligns with desired success (dream). Becoming requires time to cultivate the beliefs, values, and other internal attributes that define one's fundamental identity. Then our doing derives from who we are, our *being* so to speak. Doing happens in a creative space that is our area to dominate. When we serve what we create, in return we are compensated for being the answer to someone else's question. Therefore, our greatest being determines our greatest doing, which results in having an abundance.

Any attempt to violate the divine order will result in frustration and disappointments. Often a time, people focus on having before becoming, or focus on doing before becoming, and I am here to report that this out of divine order modus operandi will guarantee failure. True success and fulfillment springs from operating per divine order. Wise people understand that they are the engineers and architects of their inner world. Important to note is that the sole responsibility of designing the inside world that fits the picture of success one holds rests entirely on each individual.

It's the inside that originates the outside accomplishments. The success journey begins with creating your internal mindset, uniqueness, and skillset. Implying that your priority is to seek first the Kingdom within which is the root system of the wisdom tree. After which all the material stuff will be added to you, which is the fruit.

Therefore, you have to cultivate the faith on the side that will guarantee success and fulfillment. You have to cultivate a positive mental attitude on the inside. You have to operate with energy, vigor, and liveliness on the inside. Your values have to be prioritized from the most import to the least, in line with your purpose and destiny. To do this is the essential thing that will bring about the desired outcomes. Why? Because life does not give you what you want or deserve, but what you already are. Your inside is a magnet that attracts your outcomes.

Human tendency is to seek physical stuff like new house, nice car, new marriage or new address. However, acquiring new things without the right mindset, uniqueness (identity), or skillset will not bring about a new experience. If it does, it will be fleeting in nature. For instance, an old mindset or mentality in a new house and new marriage will revert to the old ways in no time. An old mind in a new car will eventually fall back into the old ways. What am saying is that if you external circumstances conflict with who you are on the inside, then the good or better things will be short lived. So it's imperative that you become on the side the person who aligns with your desired outcomes.

References

https://www.businessinsider.com/lottery-winners-lost-everything-2017

https://enduringword.com/bible-commentary/proverbs-3/

/ 7 /

WHY POVERTY IS MAN'S WILL AND NOT GOD'S PLAN

WE LIVE IN a world where poverty, pain, and suffering are commonplace. Many people resign to accepting poverty, lack, and scarcity as their fate. Worse still, is the idea or doctrine fronted by some religions that poverty is spiritual purity. Others come to terms with poverty by attributing it to God's will, which is a lazy mentality of absolving one from the responsibility of creating their own subjective world. Not forgetting the age-old question; "Why does God allow lack, scarcity, and poverty? For poverty is accompanied by pain and suffering. This question presents a theological, moral, and spiritual dilemma. Answering this question requires us to shift attention from God to mankind. David the Psalmist postulates:

> "The heaven, even the heavens, are the Lord's; but the earth He has given to the children of men."
>
> —Psalms 115:16

It is clear that earth is man's realm to govern, and heaven is God's realm. Therefore, poverty is not God's design for our lives, it's brought about by mankind's decision-making, management style, and non-conformity to God's principles. In creating man, God clearly delegated authority and responsibility for governing earth to mankind. This is corroborated by Moses the Prophet:

"Then God said, let Us make man in Our image according to our likeness; LET THEM HAVE DOMINION over the fish of the sea, over the birds of the air, and over the cattle, over all the earth and over every creeping thing that creeps on the earth."

—Genesis 1:26

It's very crystal clear from this verse, that human systems and decision-making determine outcomes in this physical realm we call earth. God chose to delegate authority and rulership over earth to man. And because God is truth, He cannot go against His Word. Intuitively, the will of God which is characterized by abundance, provision, and protection is not automatic in the earth. Otherwise, Jesus Christ wouldn't have offered us a prayer template:

"Our Father which art in heaven,
Hallowed be thy name. Thy
Kingdom come; thy will be done
in earth as it is in heaven."

—Mathew 6:9-10

Because the will of God is not automatic, mankind is responsible for inviting God into their life and let Him reign in their hearts so that they can reign over their lives or circumstances. In this physical realm we call home (for a while), spirits cannot intervene without the permission of mankind. God is spirit, and requires your permission to intervene in your domain. It's illegal and illegitimate for angels, demons, or God to intervene in man's affairs without invitation from mankind.

It's paramount to understand this principle, Why? Because God is only interested in ruling over your heart, so that you rule over your domain. Your domain could be a business or profession. God is not interested in gold, silver, money, or any material riches. He wants you to have those riches such that, if God wants money He gives it to you. Whatever God desires, He gives it you. You in whose heart, He reigns. The King of kings wants you to have the gold, silver, riches, and or material wealth, not them having you.

God is the Landlord, and we are the tenants whose earth lease expires in the end times. For now, God requires us to manage on his behalf. This is corroborated by David the Psalmist:

> "What is man that you are mindful of him, and the son of man that you visit him? For you have made him a little lower than the angels, and you have crowned him with glory and honor. You have made him to have dominion over the works of Your Hands; You have put all things under his feet."
>
> —Psalms 8: 4-6

Clearly, all things were placed under man's authority and responsibility; however, it appears that mankind is doing more mismanagement than management. God's original intention is to rule over mankind, while mankind rules over earth. But there's the flesh, the world, and the devil that time and again cause mankind to stumble. The cure to this negative influence from the world, flesh, and devil, is for man to align his heart with the truth of God, and then he becomes ruler of his circumstances. When God reigns in our hearts, we reign over our life's work.

To put this in perspective, I will allude to an example of an agreement between a landlord and tenant. For the length of time that the contract or agreement is in force, the landlord is bound by law not to access the property (his house that he owns) without the permission of the tenant. Implying that the condition of the house is now the responsibility of the tenant. How it looks like during the life of the contract reflects the tenant's management. Hence, the landlord can't be held to account for the condition of the house while the tenant is legally occupying the premises. In similar fashion, poverty and its accompanying cousins on earth derive from man's decision making and the rejection of God's principles. For its stated in Scripture:

"This Book of the law shall not depart from your mouth, but you shall meditate in it day and night. That you may observe to do according to all that is written in it. For then you will make your way prosperous, and then you will have good success."

—Joshua 1:8

Hence, not all success is good success. If success is not a result of obedience to God's law, if it's not from the guidance of the Spirit of God, and not in line with the purpose of God for your life, then that's not good success. Where there's no good success, there's no fulfillment and contentment. God's intention for mankind is a life of abundance fulfillment rooted in His presence. Right from the start, God planted the Garden of Eden, then He placed man in it with clear instructions to dress it and keep it. In the Garden, mankind's every need was met by limitless provision.

Pointing to God's blueprint of abundance, sustenance, and sufficiency premised on congruence to God's will. Scripture confirms God's desire for man's prosperity. As seen in the Book of Jeremiah:

"For I know the plans I have for you declares the Lord, plans to prosper you and not to harm you, to give you a future and a hope."

—Jeremiah 29:11

Hence, poverty is a divergence from God's perfect plan.

God's instruction to man in the Garden of Eden was "Of every tree of the garden you may freely eat." (Genesis 2:16). Intuitively, this underscores a fundamental truth in light of the will of God for our lives. That is to say, God's will for our lives is broad and wide in nature. It encompasses a variety of opportunities available to us. Growing up a Catholic, I was under the impression that God's will for my life was restrictive in nature. That I had to take extra caution in my choices and decisions so as to avoid the wrath from an angry God. I believe many Christian believers may be harboring the same if not similar sentiment. However, the good news is that you and I have an aspect of God's creative gene which is evidenced in our infinite ability to create. As gardeners, we are supposed to improve the resources at our disposal through industry, ingenuity, and productivity. You and I possess an inherent capacity to create the life we desire.

It's the reason that God endowed us with unmatched brain power, sagacity, and brilliance. The God power of the mind so to speak. We are to freely consume, but our consumption should lead to more productivity. This is true in a garden environment where consumption of fruit releases seed, which potentially leads to more fruit. Environment that is superintended by the Spirit of God is key. It is important that communion between God's Spirit and man's spirit is present, such that God reigns in our hearts as we reign of over our assignments.

The seed of creativity that lies in the fertile soils of our hearts, requires watering and nourishment by the Word of God. Not only is God's original mandate for man; "to dress and keep the garden," designates man as the gardener, but also man himself is a garden. The loam soils of our hearts possess infinite capacity for the creative seed in us to take root with the nourishment from God's Word.

In that the seed in us develops roots first by gravitropic growth. During this time we are undergoing the necessary development through knowledge, accumulation, understanding, skill acquisition, challenges withstanding to become the person to produce and sustain wealth. Trials and tests refine our mind such that we become more aware of the divine power that is at work within us. Leading to a transformation through the renewal of the mind, allowing us to receive the knowledge of truth through the conscious mind, resulting in the awakening or resurrection of the Christ awareness in our subconscious mind.

This is the fundamental truth in relation to the Kingdom of God within you. It the understanding that the Divine is awareness, that the Divine is consciousness, that the Divine is the power of thought within you. Thoughts make things, thoughts are the source of things, and as a man thinketh in his heart, so is he. You have to think rich and wealth thoughts, for wealth to manifest in your circumstances. Unfortunately, the reverse is also true.

The God in you and me does everything according to universal spiritual and physical principles. God is truth and can't violate the universal principles. This reminds me of a moment in Scripture when the devil tempted Jesus Christ to turn stones into bread.

"The tempter came to him and said, 'If you are the Son of God, tell these stones to become bread.'

"Jesus answered, 'It is written: Man shall not live on bread alone, but on every word that comes from the mouth of God.'"

—Mathew 4:3-4

The Christ in Jesus didn't oblige because doing so would have violated the fundamental principle; "The things that are seen didn't come from the things that appear (Hebrews 11:3)." In other words, things don't come from things, instead things are derived from thoughts.

Ladies and gentlemen, the mind power of thought determines the circumstances of your life. You have the power to create wealth or poverty, it's up to you.

Important to note is that you have to be intentional and deliberate in harnessing strategic thinking through use of the powers of your mind. Intentionality will give direction, conditioning, and form to the Infinite Source. However, where there's lack of intention, undesirable circumstances will be expressed in one's circumstances.

In his book, *The Hidden Power And Other Papers Upon Mental Science*, Thomas Troward postulates:

"Much has been written and said on the origin of evil, and a volume might be filled with the detailed study of the subject; but for all practical purposes it may be summed up in the one word limitation. For what is the ultimate cause of all strife, whether public or private, but the notion that the supply of good is

limited? With the bulk of
mankind this is a fixed idea, and
they therefore argue that because
there is only a certain limited
quantity of good, the share in
their possession can be increased
only by correspondingly
diminishing someone else's
share."

He goes on to add:

"If people only realized the truth
that 'good' is not a certain
limited quantity, but a stream
continuously flowing from the
exhaustless Infinite, and ready to
take any direction we choose to
give it, and that each one is able
by the action of his own thought
to draw from it indefinitely, the
substitution of this new and true
idea for the old and false one of
limitation would at one stroke
remove all strife and struggle
from the world; every man would

find a helper instead of a
competitor in every other, and
the very laws on Nature, which
now so often seem to war against
us, would be found a ceaseless
source of profit and delight."

References

The Hidden Power And Other Papers Upon Mental Science by Thomas Troward.

As A Man Thinketh by James Allen.

ONE LAST THING

ABUNDANCE IS YOUR birthright, and dominion over your circle of circumstances is by harnessing the God-power of your mind. Through self-control, love, kindness, patience, among other things, we discipline our higher intellectual factors to serve the Christ being we are. Christ consciousness is the awareness and being in tune with the Infinite Source. Which is built on the foundation of understanding the Son-to-the-Father relationship. Our task is to abandon being a prodigal son and return to the Father, who says to us that all I have is yours;

to know the Father is in you, and you are in the father; and to know that you and the Father are one.

This is the center piece of Jesus Christ's teaching. Ladies and gentlemen, may the Christ in you please stand up, stand out, and stand firm.

The Christ in you is the Universal Principle for the congruence of the superconscious, conscious, and subconscious mind. It's what Max Maltz refers to as Psycho-Cybernetics. Others call it the Law of the Mind. But the important thing lies in understanding and recognizing the presence of Christ in you. I am talking about the awareness of the Christ in you. Wisdom is the fundamental truth that you and Christ (God, The Father, The Source) are one, and that Christ is in you, and you are in Christ. Know that the Father is in you, and you are in the Father, that you and the Father are one, recognizing that you are the Christ, the Son of the Living God.

You have to be in tune with the Infinite Source (The Father) through faith, and embrace the co-existence of this Divine truth. With this awareness you will be operating from an abundance consciousness. When it comes to this fundamental truth, I can only point you to it, but can't give it to you. Even Jesus Christ, the greatest Teacher would only point us to and in the direction of the Truth (The Kingdom of God within you). You will have to discover it, gain revelation of it, and experience it.

Whatever thoughts preoccupy you, they have to transform into things. Every thought in your mind becomes a thing, therefore be transformed by the renewing of your mind. There's no greater Lord of lords than your mind. You serve your mind, and it serves you.

"Thus says the Lord, ask me of things to come concerning my sons, and concerning the work of my hands command ye me."

—Isaiah 45:11

The Lord that is your mind, your thoughts, your imagination is waiting on your commands. Paul the Apostle put it this way:

"The person without the Spirit does not accept the things that come from the Spirit of God but considers them foolishness, and cannot understand them because they are discerned only through the Spirit."

—1 Corinthians 2:14

When you embrace the fundamental Truth of the Divine in you, and you in the Divine, and that you co-exist with the Divine, that is the epitome of wisdom. Implying that you are limitless and infinitely wealth since you are in tune with the Source of all things. All that the Father has is yours. Just remember, as a man thinketh so is he. Just like a child born into royalty has to be trained to become a prince, you too are born in Divine royalty, and have to be transformed by the renewing of your mind. You have the mind of Christ.

"For, 'Who can know the LORD's thoughts? Who knows enough to teach him?' But we understand these things, for we have the mind of Christ."

—1 Corinthian 2:16

You have to train your mind such that it undergoes soul development. For your mind has twelve great power entities residing in your subconscious. These are functional attributes or centers of action that by nature are egos or identities. You see after He attained a certain soul development, Jesus the personal consciousness called His twelve apostles to Him. What this means is that a man reaches a point and develops out of mere personal consciousness into a spiritual consciousness (super consciousness), the Christ so to speak. How? By discipling the great twelve powers through a deeper inner reflection via thought, and which thoughts are made alive by the spoken word.

Prior to spiritual consciousness, one is limited in their abilities due to the finiteness of the ego identity. However, with the resurrection of the twelve powers through a deeper spiritual awareness, one is infinitely unlimited in their ability due to the Oneness with the Source (The Father).

Wealth in life is purchased with the currency of self-awareness. Self-awareness or self-consciousness is also self-identity which defines the boundaries of one's being, doing, and having. Believe you me, the first and second coming of Christ is spoken of in the Scriptures, is the mind transformation from personal consciousness to spiritual consciousness. The first coming is the receiving of truth in the conscious mind, while the second coming is the awareness through the resurrection of the subconscious mind into the mind of Christ (the spiritual intelligence).

True wealth lies in embracing this fundamental Truth. You can only express these twelve powers through the guidance of the Divine Mind.

References

Psycho-Cybernetics by Maxwell Maltz, MD

As A Man Thinketh by James Allen

The Hidden Power And Other Papers Upon Mental Science by Thomas Troward.

https://www.truthunity.net/books/the-twelve-powers-of-man-15-23

ABOUT THE
AUTHOR

ROBERT MULINDWA was born and raised in
Uganda, the Pearl of Africa. He currently lives
in Nashville, Tennessee USA. Robert's writing
is predicated on the idea that each person is
born for a purpose with potential or hidden
capacity to fulfill their reason for existence.

Robert is holder of a Statistics and Math
degree in undergraduate studies, as well as a
postgraduate degree in Financial Management

and Investment. Robert is also a trained and licensed registered nurse (RN).

Created for Success: Finding God's Will, Our Purpose, & True Happiness is his first book.

To reach Robert about speaking, appearances, quantity discounts on books, and other matters, please visit:

www.RobertMulindwa.com

SUBSCRIBE TODAY TO ROBERT'S

FREE NEWSLETTER

Subscribe today to get occasional updates and I will send you chapters 1-3 of my book, *Created for Success.*

www.RobertMulindwa.com

OTHER BOOKS
BY ROBERT MULINDWA

CREATED *for* SUCCESS

IN A WORLD where
success seems based
on comparison and
impressions, we only
find true and
genuine success after
we first find our
reason for being
here. Discovery and
fulfillment of
purpose is what true
success, fulfillment,
and contentment are

about. And we only need connect what is
within us with Holy Spirit guidance.

Get your copy today.

www.RobertMulindwa.com

REDISCOVERING IDENTITY

In *Rediscovering Identity*, author Robert Mulindwa expounds on why it's paramount and essential to understand one's true identity. Only when one asks the most important question, "Who am I?" can one rightfully address the

crucial and equally important question of, "Why am I here?" Understanding one's identity as the image of God creates an awareness in one's mind that they are a spirit with a soul living in a physical body.

Get your copy today.

www.RobertMulindwa.com

THANK YOU

I SINCERELY HOPE you enjoyed *Gain Wisdom, Gain Wealth* as much as I enjoyed writing it, and that it does help you achieve a more successful future, one guided by God's will and filled with fulfilment and purpose.

You could have picked any book, but you picked mine, and for that I'm grateful. I hope it added value and quality to your life. If so, it would be really nice if you could share this book with your colleagues, friends, and family. It may help them as well. You might post a review or your thoughts on Amazon, Facebook, Twitter, and/or simply recommend it to someone.

Your feedback and support will help me improve my craft and fill my heart.

Thank you!

Robert Mulindwa

www.ingramcontent.com/pod-product-compliance
Lightning Source LLC
Chambersburg PA
CBHW021153130626
46554CB00005B/1801